The ● Haeger NaturalStone™
pizza
COOKBOOK

recipes Brigit Binns

photographs David Matheson

Contents

Making Pizza at Home

Pizza is Italian in origin, but this humble flatbread with savory toppings has captured the attention of the entire planet. Pizza is enjoyed across the globe, and in every country where it's eaten it's tailored to the cultural palate.

In Italy, pizza is made with a great deal of restraint and respect for tradition. Pizza Napoletana—or Neapolitan pizza—is widely regarded as the best pizza in the world, so much so that it's been given special, governmental status to protect its integrity. This means that only pizzas made according to certain strict standards can be called authentic Neapolitan pizza. There are two primary types of traditional Neapolitan pizza: marinara pizza made with tomato sauce, garlic, and oregano, and Margherita pizza made with fresh tomatoes, fresh mozzarella, and basil.

In contrast to the Italian approach, in the United Sates and elsewhere across the world, many liberties have been taken with the creation of pizza. Popular American pies include barbecued chicken pizza with smoky, tangy barbecue sauce; Hawaiian pizza topped with pineapple and Canadian bacon; and "The Works," a pizza blanketed with every imaginable topping. Then there are the regional pizzas: New York is known for its thin-crust pizza and Chicago for its deep-dish pies. Devotees of each will argue passionately about which is the best.

Pizza is often considered convenience food because it's usually ordered out. Homemade pizza, however, is not about convenience—it's about enjoying the making and baking process, as well as the satisfaction that goes along with creating wholesome and delicious food. To help get you started with pizza-baking at home, this book contains all the recipes you need. It covers Italian classics like Margherita Pizza (page 34); American favorites like Pepperoni Pizza (page 47); inspired pies like Jerk Chicken Pizza with Smoked Gouda and Red Onion (page 52); and pizza spin-offs, such as stromboli (page 71). You will also find recipes for a variety of doughs and pizza staples like tomato sauce and pesto.

Haeger NaturalStone™ is perfectly suited for all your pizza-baking needs. Made from natural clays mined in Kentucky and Tennessee, this bakeware is durable and has heating capabilities up to 450°F. It is safe for use in the oven and microwave, moves with versatility from oven to table for ease in serving, and is dishwasher safe for easy cleanup. While the shape of this bakeware is ideal for baking round pizzas, it also does a great job of baking other items such as cookies, pies, chicken, vegetables and more. For more ideas on how to use your Haeger NaturalStone™ bakeware, turn to page 75.

Pizza equipment

PIZZA STONE

Traditionally, pizzas are baked in coal- or wood-fired ovens with brick floors that produce crisp, brown crusts. To imitate the intense heat of a brick oven in a home oven, a pizza stone—a flat piece of unglazed stoneware—works beautifully. Haeger NaturalStone™ pizza stones have a composition that absorbs and retains heat so that the oven temperature does not drop drastically each time the oven door is opened, ensuring that your pizza is evenly baked.

Before your first use, wash your new NaturalStone™ pizza stone by hand in hot water. Always allow stoneware to cool to room temperature prior to washing. The all-natural stone will season over time, creating an easy-release surface that requires little cleaning: Just soak the stone in hot water for 15 minutes to remove most, or all, of the baked-on food. Food still clinging to the surface can be scrubbed off with a nylon cleaning pad and warm water (soap may be used, but make sure to rinse thoroughly). The stoneware is also dishwasher safe. See opposite and turn to page 16 for more on baking pizza with a NaturalStone™ pizza stone.

Do not use stoneware that is chipped, has visible cracks, or is damaged in any way.

A pizza peel, sometimes called a baker's peel, is a wide paddle made of wood or metal, attached to a long handle. It's used to slide freeform pizzas and breads onto and off of a hot pizza stone because it's usually too treacherous to handle the heavy pizza stone itself. Haeger pizza stones are relatively lightweight, and are designed with side handles that make it easy to transfer the stone into and out of the oven, so a pizza peel is not necessary.

KNIVES AND CUTTERS

A chef's knife is an indispensable kitchen tool for any cook, pizza-bakers included. It's not only used for preparing the ingredients that go on top of a pizza, it's also useful for cutting the baked pizza for serving. To slice your pizza, use the largest chef's knife you own, preferably one with an 8- to 10-inch blade. Place the tip of the knife at the center of the pie with the knife handle angled upward. Press down on the back of the upper part of the blade with your other hand to steady the blade and make sure that the tip of the knife cuts through the bottom crust. Lower the knife handle to cut through the pie; before removing the knife, make sure that you have cut all the way through the bottom crust. Repeat to cut the rest of the pizza. For some shape variety, you can cut oval or rectangular pizzas into strips, rectangles, or squares.

For slicing baked pizzas, a pizza wheel is not a necessity, but it's a handy tool to have, especially if you make pizza often. With one quick movement, a pizza wheel allows you to cut cleanly through the toppings and crust. When shopping, look for a solidly built pizza wheel with a comfortable, secure grip and a large, sturdy blade.

DOUGH-MAKING EQUIPMENT

Pizza dough is easy to make and comes together quickly in a food processor or in a heavy-duty stand mixer with a dough hook attachment. The recipes in this book were developed using an 11-cup food processor, but you can also use a heavy-duty stand mixer for mixing and kneading dough in one easy step. For more on making pizza dough, turn to page 12.

Getting the most out of your Haeger NaturalStone™ pizza stone

Follow these simple guidelines to maximize the effectiveness and longevity of your pizza stone, and to ensure your own safety. Care for and use your pizza stone properly, and you'll be turning out restaurant-quality pizzas with perfectly crisped crusts every time.

- Thoroughly read the use and care instructions that came with your Haeger NaturalStone™ pizza stone.

- Before your first use, wash your new NaturalStone™ pizza stone by hand in hot water and let dry completely before using.

- Preheat the oven, but do not preheat the Haeger NaturalStone™ bakeware. The oven temperature should not exceed 450°F.

- Do not use stoneware under a broiler or on any stove-top burner or direct heat source, like a grill.

- Unlike traditional pizza stones, do not leave the pizza stone in the oven when not in use.

- NaturalStone™ performs best in conventional and convection ovens. Convection ovens may require less time and a lower temperature setting than standard ovens.

- Do not add water or apply any liquid after your pizza stone has been heated or while in the oven.

- Avoid extreme temperature changes.

- Always use a dry, heat-resistant oven mitt or dry heat-resistant pads when handling your hot pizza stone.

- After baking, always place a hot pizza stone on a dry, heat-resistant surface to prevent temperature shock and to protect your counter or tabletop from heat and scratching.

- Always allow NaturalStone™ stoneware to cool to room temperature prior to washing.

- If you have baked-on food, soaking stoneware in hot water for 15 minutes will release most of it. If you have stubborn food to remove, use a nylon cleaning pad to finish, then rinse and air dry.

- Soap may be used when washing, but make sure to rinse thoroughly. NaturalStone™ is also dishwasher safe.

- Avoid dropping or bumping NaturalStone™ stoneware as it may break, chip, or crack. If your stoneware is damaged in any way, handle it with care. Broken stoneware pieces may be sharp and if handled improperly may cause injury. Using protective gloves, carefully place them in a carton and dispose of safely.

- Do not use stoneware that is chipped, has visible cracks or is damaged in any way.

Pizza ingredients

DOUGH INGREDIENTS

Just a handful of basic ingredients is all that is needed to make pizza dough at home. All-purpose flour, a kitchen staple, is the foundation for almost all of the pizza doughs in this book. All-purpose flour is often bleached to produce a pure white color, but this bleaching process also adversely affects flavor. Unbleached all-purpose flour has a fuller, nuttier, more complex flavor than bleached all-purpose flour. The dough recipes in this book that call for all-purpose flour were developed using the unbleached variety. Sturdy bread flour, nutty-flavored whole-wheat flour, and hearty semolina flour are the other types of flour that are used to make pizza doughs. These doughs can be used interchangeably with the basic dough.

Yeast is a microorganism that is used to naturally leaven breads—that is, get them to rise so that they bake up with airy, open structures. With the exception of the Semolina Pizza Dough (page 21), which uses active dry yeast, the dough recipes in this book were developed using quick-rise yeast; both types are commonly available in grocery stores. They are not interchangeable, so be sure to use the exact type of yeast called for.

Salt heightens and improves the flavor of any food to which it is added, including pizza dough. For pizza dough, it's best to use fine- to medium-grained salt—such as table salt and kosher salt—so that the granules will be easily and evenly distributed throughout.

Just a small measure of olive oil gives pizza dough richness as well as some suppleness. It's not necessary to use your finest extra-virgin olive oil to make pizza dough, but do try to use an olive oil with good flavor.

TOPPING INGREDIENTS

It goes without saying: To create the most flavorful pizzas, use the best-quality and freshest ingredients that you can find. Salt and pepper—the most basic of seasonings—go a long way in adding flavor. A few recipes in this book call specifically for coarse sea salt as a topping because it adds texture and bursts of saltiness. Freshly ground black peppercorns offer the fullest, spiciest black-pepper flavor.

Look for authentic cheeses at cheesemongers or specialty food stores that sell their stock quickly so that you're assured the freshest cheese. In the case of Parmesan, a good grating and eating cheese to keep on hand, it's best to purchase only as much as you plan to use in a couple of weeks so that it doesn't dry out or turn moldy. Grate or shred cheese yourself at home instead of buying the pre-grated or pre-shredded varieties. Use Parmigiano-Reggiano (true Parmesan cheese made near Parma in Northern Italy) for the best flavor.

Try to purchase produce from local growers or farmers' markets. Tomatoes should be plump, vibrant in color, and blemish free. Heads of garlic should be tight, firm, and without green shoots sprouting from the tops of the cloves. Fresh herbs should be bright green and possess a heady fragrance. Some recipes in this book call for dried herbs because they offer a unique flavor profile that is particularly suited to pizza. Make sure that the dried herbs from your pantry are flavorful and fragrant.

Some of the pizza recipes call for drizzling the baked pizza with olive oil just before serving to add luster and flavor. This is the time to use your fine extra-virgin olive oil with rich, fruity flavor.

Making the dough

WORKING WITH YEAST

Most of the dough recipes in this book call for quick-rise yeast, which can be added directly to the other dough ingredients. Active dry yeast, however, must be "proofed" before it can be used.

To proof active dry yeast, sprinkle it over warm water (about 110°F) in a bowl or measuring cup; adding a little bit of sugar helps to activate the yeast more quickly. Upon standing for 5–10 minutes, the yeast should become foamy. (UPPER LEFT) If it doesn't become foamy, the yeast is most likely dead and unusable. It's best to start over with new active dry yeast.

MAKING THE DOUGH

A food processor makes quick work of making pizza dough—with just a few quick pulses and less than a minute of processing, the dough is formed. The doughs in this book were developed using an 11-cup food processor. (A smaller machine cannot handle the dough quantity.) In a food processor, the dry ingredients are pulsed together and the liquids are added while the machine is running. The dough will come together in a rough mass. Let it rest for 5–10 minutes and then process it again for about 30 seconds more to fully develop the protein and make the dough resilient. (UPPER RIGHT)

You can also make pizza dough in a standing mixer: Fit the mixer with the dough hook attachment and follow the basic food processor procedure; however, the mixing times for a standing mixer will be significantly longer. The final knead, after the 5–10 minute rest, should result in a smooth, elastic dough and can take up to 10 minutes.

No matter how you make the dough, once it is kneaded, it should be soft and smooth and should feel moist and slightly tacky to the touch, but not at all wet or sticky.

LETTING THE DOUGH RISE

During rising, the dough develops the complex flavors and texture that are characteristic of yeasted breads. Place the dough in a lightly oiled bowl and then turn the dough over so that the top is lightly coated with oil. Cover the bowl with plastic wrap or a clean kitchen towel. The film of oil will prevent the surface of the dough from drying out as it rises. A draft-free spot is ideal for allowing the dough to rise; warmth will cause it to rise quickly, and cool temperatures will slow it down. When the dough is puffy and has doubled in volume, which takes about 1½ hours in a warm spot, it is ready to use. (BOTTOM LEFT)

DIVIDING THE DOUGH

Turn the risen dough out onto a lightly floured work surface and gently punch it down to knock out the air. Work the dough into a cylinder of even thickness. (This shape is easy to divide evenly.) Using a chef's knife, cut the cylinder in half, or as directed in the recipe. Shape each piece of dough into a ball by cupping your hands around its sides and moving the dough along the work surface in a circular motion; the dough's tackiness against the surface should help pull it into a compact ball (BOTTOM RIGHT) that will be easy to roll or stretch out into an even round. If you are using only one piece of dough, as most of the recipes in this book specify, place the extra dough ball in a gallon-size zipper-lock plastic bag, press out the air, and seal it well. Freeze the dough for up to 2 months; let it thaw at room temperature for 3–4 hours before use.

Shaping and topping your pizza

SHAPING THE DOUGH ROUND

For most pizzas, your hands are all you will need in order to shape the dough. Hand-formed pizzas have more character than those made by machine in high-volume pizzeria—they have slightly irregular shapes and are more likely to bake up with appealing bubbles because not all the air is pressed out of the dough as it is when the dough is rolled with a rolling pin.

Set the dough on a lightly floured work surface. Coat your fingers with olive oil to prevent them from sticking to the dough. Then, using your palms and fingers, push, pat, and press the dough outward from the center, leaving the edge slightly thicker. (UPPER LEFT)

If, while you shape the dough, it becomes elastic and shrinks back, cover it with a kitchen towel and allow it to rest for about 15 minutes before proceeding. Resting gives the gluten—the protein in the flour that was developed during kneading—a chance to relax so that the dough is more workable. If, in the end, your pie turns out misshapen, don't worry—such imperfections make a pizza look rustic and handcrafted.

ALLOWING THE DOUGH ROUND TO RISE

After shaping the dough, cover it with a clean kitchen towel and let it rise on the work surface for about 15 minutes. This brief second rise before the dough is topped allows it to develop just a little bit of volume so that it doesn't bake up heavy and dense. (UPPER RIGHT)

OILING AND SEASONING THE DOUGH ROUND

After the second rise and before topping the dough, carefully transfer the dough round to the pizza stone.

You may need to pull out the edges to help reform it in a circular shape. Brush the edges or the entire round with olive oil. This light coating of oil helps the edges bake up golden brown and crisp. It is not necessary to use extra-virgin olive oil here—regular olive oil does a fine job. (BOTTOM LEFT)

Before being topped, the dough round is often seasoned with salt and pepper. This helps bring the flavors of the crust and toppings together and heightens the flavor of each bite. (BOTTOM RIGHT)

TOPPING THE DOUGH ROUND

Authentic Neapolitan pizzas are topped with a light hand, allowing the flavorful crust to share the spotlight with the toppings. The pizzas in this book follow this Italian-style approach. To top the pizza, layer the desired toppings on the dough round, usually beginning with a moderate amount of sauce. Leave a 1/2-inch border free so that the pizza bakes up with a crisp, brown edge. If you're opting to use your own selection of toppings, make sure that they are not very heavy or wet, which will cause the crust to bake up soggy and doughy.

STORING EXTRA DOUGH

The dough recipes in the Pizza Basics chapter make enough dough to form two regular pies, but most of the pizza recipes make enough topping for only one pie. You can store the second dough ball in a zipper-lock bag in the refrigerator overnight, or, for longer storage, freeze it for up to 2 months. (Thaw frozen dough at room temperature for 3–4 hours before using.)

Baking pizza

Neapolitan and commercial pizza ovens reach very high temperatures, usually in excess of 700°F. With such high heat, thin-crust pizzas bake in just a couple of minutes. Home ovens don't generate this kind of intense heat, which is why it is important to use a pizza stone. Using a Haeger NaturalStone™ pizza stone, your thin-crust pizza should be done in 18–20 minutes, but every oven will call for slightly different baking times. For thicker pizzas and for filled variations on pizza, such as calzone (page 68) and stromboli (page 71), lower oven temperatures and longer cooking times ensure that the interiors bake through without the exteriors scorching.

Haeger NaturalStone™ pizza stones are oven-safe up to 450°F, but should not be placed over any direct heat source, such as a broiler, stove-top burner, or grill, and should not be preheated in the oven. NaturalStone™ performs best in conventional and convection ovens. (Note that convection ovens may require less time and a lower temperature than standard ovens.)

The easiest way to get your pizza into the oven is to put the dough round on top of the pizza stone and then add the toppings, distributing the items evenly over the cooking surface. When you are ready to bake the pizza, using the side handles, carefully transfer the pizza stone to the oven. Bake the pizza until the crust is golden and crisp and the cheese is bubbling. You can use a long-handled spatula to lift an edge of the pizza just slightly so you can check the bottom of the crust. Keep a close watch on the pizza to avoid a burnt crust.

To remove the pizza from the oven, using heat-resistant oven mitts, carefully grasp the side handles of the pizza stone and transfer the stone to a dry, heat-resistant surface to cool slightly before cutting. You can cut your pizza directly on the Haeger NaturalStone™ pizza stone.

In general, pizza is best hot out of the oven, with only a minute or two of rest to allow the toppings to cool down slightly so that they will not slide off when the pieces are pulled apart. Delicate herbs and a last-minute drizzle of extra-virgin olive oil are put on the pizza right at the end, just before it is cut, to add fresh color and flavor.

Let the stone cool completely before using it again, or before soaking or washing it, and do not leave it in the oven when not in use.

Thinking beyond pizza

While the round shape of the Haeger NaturalStone™ bakeware is ideally suited for baking pizza, it also does a great job with a variety of other types of baked items. Cookies, scones, biscuits, galettes (flat, fruit-filled pies), and other dough-based foods come out crisp and golden brown when baked on Haeger NaturalStone™ bakeware. You can also bake savory recipes with success, such as oven-baked chicken strips, roasted summer vegetables, and stuffed portobello mushroom caps. Turn to page 75 for these recipes and more.

One important thing to remember when using the NaturalStone™ bakeware is to be sure to cover at least two-thirds of the surface area of the stone with the food items in order to ensure even baking. When using the bakeware with other recipes, you may need to add additional minutes to the baking time, epecially if your recipe bakes for less than 15 minutes.

Pizza Basics

Pizza Dough

3⅓ cups all-purpose flour, plus extra for dusting

¼ cup whole-wheat flour

1 package (2½ tsp) quick-rise yeast

1 tbsp sugar

1 tbsp salt

1¼ cups warm water (110°F), plus extra as needed

2 tbsp olive oil, plus extra as needed

In a food processor, combine the all-purpose flour, whole-wheat flour, yeast, sugar, and salt. Pulse to mix the ingredients. With the motor running, add the water and olive oil in a steady stream, and then pulse until the dough comes together in a rough mass, about 12 seconds. If the dough does not form into a ball, sprinkle with 1–2 teaspoons of water and pulse again until a rough mass forms. Let the dough rest for 5–10 minutes. Process again for 25–30 seconds, steadying the top of the food processor with one hand. The dough should be tacky to the touch but not sticky. Transfer the dough to a lightly floured work surface and form it into a smooth ball. Place the dough in a large oiled bowl, turn to coat with oil, and cover with plastic wrap. Let the dough rise in a warm place until doubled in bulk and spongy (see page 12), about 1½ hours.

Turn the dough out onto a lightly floured work surface, punch it down, and shape into a smooth cylinder. Divide the dough into 2 equal pieces. Shape each piece into a smooth ball, dusting with flour only if the dough becomes sticky. Cover both balls of dough with a clean kitchen towel and let rest for 10 minutes before proceeding with your chosen pizza recipe. If you are using only one ball of dough, place the second ball in a gallon-size zipper-lock bag and freeze for up to 2 months. (When ready to use, thaw the frozen dough for 3–4 hours at room temperature.)

MAKES 2 BALLS OF DOUGH

This versatile pizza dough can be used to make many different types of pizza, including calzone and stromboli. When shaping a pizza, keep in mind that the thinner the dough is stretched, the crisper the crust will be.

Semolina Pizza Dough

In a measuring pitcher, stir together the warm water and the sugar and sprinkle with the yeast. Let the mixture stand until it starts to foam, about 5 minutes. Add the 1 cup room-temperature water and the olive oil.

In a food processor, combine the semolina flour, all-purpose flour, and salt. With the motor running, add the yeast-water mixture in a steady stream, and then pulse until the dough comes together in a rough mass, about 12 seconds. If the dough does not form into a ball, sprinkle with 1–2 teaspoons of water and pulse again until a rough mass forms. Let rest for 5–10 minutes. Process again for 25–30 seconds, steadying the top of the food processor with one hand. The dough should be tacky to the touch but not sticky. Transfer the dough to a lightly floured work surface and form it into a smooth ball. Place the dough in a large oiled bowl, turn to coat with oil, and cover with plastic wrap. Let the dough rise in a warm place until doubled in bulk and spongy (see page 12), about 1½ hours.

Turn the dough out onto a lightly floured work surface, punch it down, and shape into a smooth cylinder. Divide the dough into 2 equal pieces. Shape each piece into a smooth ball, dusting with flour only if the dough becomes sticky. Cover both balls of dough with a clean kitchen towel and let rest for 10 minutes before proceeding with your chosen pizza recipe. If you are using only one ball of dough, place the second ball in a gallon-size zipper-lock bag and freeze for up to 2 months. (When ready to use, thaw the frozen dough for 3–4 hours at room temperature.)

MAKES 2 BALLS OF DOUGH

¼ cup warm water (110°F)

1 tsp sugar

1 package (2½ tsp) active dry yeast

1 cup room-temperature water, plus extra as needed

1 tbsp olive oil, plus extra as needed

2 cups plus 2 tbsp fine semolina flour

1 cup plus 7 tbsp all-purpose flour, plus extra for dusting

1 tbsp salt

Semolina is a protein-rich flour that makes this dough resilient and gives the baked crust a chewy, tooth-sinking texture. Semolina dough is ideal for Egg, Sausage & Cheese Breakfast Pizzas (page 62) and Meatball Pizza (page 67).

Whole-Wheat Pizza Dough

In a food processor, combine the all-purpose flour, whole-wheat flour, yeast, salt, and sugar. Pulse to mix the ingredients. With the motor running, add the water and olive oil in a steady stream, and then pulse until the dough comes together in a rough mass, about 12 seconds. If the dough does not form into a ball, sprinkle with 1–2 teaspoons of water and pulse again until a rough mass forms. Let rest for 5–10 minutes. Process again for 25–30 seconds, steadying the top of the food processor with one hand. The dough should be tacky to the touch but not sticky. Transfer the dough to a lightly floured work surface and form it into a smooth ball. Place the dough in a large oiled bowl, turn to coat with oil, and cover with plastic wrap. Let the dough rise in a warm place until doubled in bulk and spongy (see page 12), about 1½ hours.

Turn the dough out onto a lightly floured work surface, punch it down, and knead into a smooth cylinder. Divide the dough into 2 equal pieces. Shape each piece into a smooth ball, dusting with flour only if the dough becomes sticky. Cover both balls of dough with a clean kitchen towel and let rest for 10 minutes before proceeding with your chosen pizza recipe. If you are using only one ball of dough, place the second ball in a gallon-size zipper-lock bag and freeze for up to 2 months. (When ready to use, thaw the frozen dough for 3–4 hours at room temperature.)

MAKES 2 BALLS OF DOUGH

2¼ cups all-purpose flour, plus extra for dusting

1⅓ cups whole-wheat flour

1 package (2½ tsp) quick-rise yeast

2 tsp salt

1 tsp sugar

1¼ cups warm water (110°F), plus extra as needed

2 tbsp olive oil, plus extra as needed

The trick to delicious whole-wheat pizza dough is adding enough whole-wheat flour to give the crust rich, nutty flavor, but not so much that it bakes up heavy and dense. This recipe strikes a perfect balance and can be used to make almost any type of pizza.

Simple Tomato Sauce

¼ cup olive oil

5 cloves garlic, minced

1 can (15 oz) crushed tomatoes

1 tsp dried basil

¾ tsp dried oregano

¼ tsp dried thyme

¼ tsp freshly ground pepper

1½–2 tbsp red wine vinegar

Salt

In a small frying pan over medium heat, warm the olive oil. Add the garlic and cook, stirring frequently, until fragrant, 1–2 minutes. Be careful not to let it scorch or the garlic will taste bitter.

In a bowl, stir together the garlic-oil mixture, tomatoes, basil, oregano, thyme, pepper, ⅓ cup of water, and 1½ tablespoons of the vinegar. Season to taste with salt and additional vinegar. Use right away or refrigerate in an airtight container for up to 1 week.

MAKES ABOUT 2¾ CUPS

Canned tomatoes vary in salt content, so to start, season the sauce with just a pinch of salt and then gradually add more to taste. When seasoning with the red wine vinegar, add just enough to make the flavor really sparkle; the sauce shouldn't taste too tangy.

Black Olive Tapenade

1²⁄₃ cups brine-cured black olives

3 anchovy fillets

3 tbsp capers, rinsed and drained

3 cloves garlic, finely chopped

1¹⁄₂ tbsp brandy

3 tbsp fresh lemon juice

¹⁄₂ tsp freshly ground white pepper

¹⁄₄ cup extra-virgin olive oil

1¹⁄₂ tbsp coarsely chopped fresh flat-leaf parsley leaves

On a cutting board, spread the olives in a single layer. Lay the flat side of the blade of a chef's knife on top of the olives and, applying pressure with your hand, gently crush the olives so that the flesh splits. Using your fingers, remove and discard the olive pits.

Rinse the anchovy fillets and pat them dry with paper towels.

In a food processor, combine the olives, anchovies, capers, garlic, brandy, lemon juice, and white pepper. Pulse once or twice to chop roughly, and then add the olive oil and pulse briefly until combined, scraping down the sides of the bowl once or twice. The texture should be chunky. Transfer the mixture to a bowl and stir in the parsley. Use right away or refrigerate in an airtight container for up to 2 days.

MAKES ABOUT 1³⁄₄ CUPS

This rustic, chunky spread is full of bold Mediterranean flavors. To be true to tapenade's Provençal roots, make it using the tiny, relatively mild-tasting Niçoise olives.

Sun-Dried Tomato Pesto

If you are using dry-packed sun-dried tomatoes, place them in a heatproof bowl and cover them with hot water. Let them soak until soft and pliable, about 20 minutes. Drain the sun-dried tomatoes and squeeze them to remove excess moisture. (If you are using oil-packed sun-dried tomatoes, you can skip this step.)

In a food processor, combine the sun-dried tomatoes, thyme, and 1–2 tablespoons olive oil. Process to a smooth paste, adding more olive oil, as needed, until a thick, spreadable mixture forms, about 20 seconds, scraping down the sides of the bowl once or twice. Use right away or refrigerate in an airtight container for up to 1 week.

MAKES ABOUT ½ CUP

½ cup dry-packed or oil-packed sun-dried tomatoes

½ tsp fresh thyme leaves

Extra-virgin olive oil, as needed

Sun-dried tomatoes contain the concentrated sweet-tart essence of red, ripe tomatoes. If you're opting to use dry-packed sun-dried tomatoes, look for ones that feel moist, plump, and pliant, a good indicator that the tomatoes are fresh.

Basil Pesto

To toast the pine nuts, in a small dry frying pan, warm the pine nuts over medium heat, shaking the pan occasionally, until fragrant and lightly browned, 2–3 minutes. Transfer the nuts to a plate and let cool to room temperature.

Fill a saucepan with water, bring to a boil over high heat, and season lightly with salt. Add the basil and let cook for 10 seconds, remove with a slotted spoon, and plunge into a bowl of ice water. Let stand for 1 minute to halt the cooking. Remove the basil from the ice bath and squeeze the leaves dry with your hands to remove as much excess moisture as possible.

In a food processor, combine the toasted pine nuts, basil, garlic, olive oil, and 1/8 teaspoon sea salt. Process for about 30 seconds, scraping down the sides of the bowl once or twice. Add the cheese and process until combined, about 5 seconds more. Season to taste with additional sea salt. Use right away or refrigerate in an airtight container for up to 2 days.

MAKES ABOUT 1 CUP

2 tbsp pine nuts

Table salt

2½ cups fresh basil leaves

5 garlic cloves, coarsely chopped

¾ cup extra-virgin olive oil

Fine sea salt

2 tbsp grated Parmesan cheese

Salty, savory Black Olive Tapenade (top left, page 26); sweet, intense Sun-Dried Tomato Pesto (center, page 27); and herbal, garlicky Basil Pesto (bottom) are all easy-to-make toppings that add rich and robust flavors to your pizzas.

Caramelized Onions

2 tbsp olive oil

2 small yellow onions, halved lengthwise and thinly sliced

1 clove garlic, minced

Salt and freshly ground pepper

In a cast-iron or nonstick frying pan over medium-low heat, warm the oil. Add the onions and 1 tablespoon of water, cover, and cook, stirring occasionally, until softened, about 20 minutes. Uncover and cook, stirring more frequently, until much of the liquid has evaporated and the onions are slightly golden, 5–10 minutes more. Be careful not to let them scorch.

Stir in the garlic and cook until fragrant and combined, about 1 minute. Season to taste with salt and pepper. Use right away or refrigerate in an airtight container for up to 1 day.

MAKES ABOUT 1¼ CUPS

These caramelized onions get a decidedly savory edge from the addition of a clove of garlic stirred in at the end of cooking. You can use sweet varieties here, such as Vidalia onions, but they will caramelize much more quickly because they contain more sugar.

Marinated Roasted Peppers

If you are using a fresh red bell pepper, roast the pepper over a gas flame, turning occasionally with tongs, until the skin is blistered and blackened, but not ashy, all over, 4–6 minutes. Alternatively, broil the pepper under a preheated broiler about 2 inches from the heat, turning every 5 minutes, until the skin is blistered and blackened, but not ashy, all over, 15–20 minutes. Transfer the pepper to a bowl and cover tightly with plastic wrap. Let stand for 10–15 minutes. Slide the skin off with your fingers or a clean kitchen towel. Remove and discard the stem. (If you are using a jarred bell pepper, you can skip this step.)

Place the bell pepper on a cutting board and cut it so that it lies flat. Remove and discard the seeds and ribs, and then cut the pepper into thin strips.

In a bowl, stir together the olive oil, garlic, and oregano. Add the pepper strips and toss to coat. Season to taste with salt and pepper. Let the peppers marinate for at least 30 minutes or for up to 1 hour at room temperature. Use right away or refrigerate in an airtight container for up to 4 days.

MAKES ABOUT 1 CUP

1 large red bell pepper or 1 large jarred fire-roasted red bell pepper

1 tbsp olive oil

1 large clove garlic, minced

¼ tsp dried oregano

Salt and freshly ground pepper

Plain roasted bell peppers are a good pizza topping, but marinating in garlic and herbs really punches up their flavor and makes them outstanding. If you're using jarred roasted peppers, look for whole ones; if they're unavailable, use 1 cup of pepper pieces.

Classic Pizzas

Margherita Pizza

1 ball Pizza Dough
(page 20), at room
temperature

All-purpose flour
for dusting

Olive oil for shaping
and brushing

3 plum tomatoes or 2 large
vine-ripened tomatoes,
sliced ¼ inch thick

3 oz fresh mozzarella,
sliced and then torn into
bite-sized pieces

Salt and freshly
ground pepper

3–4 large fresh basil leaves,
torn into small pieces

Extra-virgin olive oil
for drizzling

Place a rack in the center of the oven and preheat to 450°F.

Place the dough ball on a lightly floured work surface. Coat your fingers with olive oil and press the dough outward from the center into a 12-inch round with a slightly raised edge (see page 15). If the dough springs back, cover it with a clean kitchen towel and let it rest for a few minutes, then continue. Cover the finished dough round with a clean kitchen towel and let rise for 15 minutes.

Carefully transfer the dough round to the pizza stone. Brush the raised edge of the dough with a light coating of olive oil. Arrange the sliced tomatoes over the dough so that they are almost touching one another, leaving a ½-inch border uncovered. Top with the mozzarella. Season lightly with salt and pepper. Transfer the pizza stone to the oven. Bake until the crust is golden brown and the cheese is bubbling, 18–20 minutes.

Using oven mitts, carefully remove the pizza stone from the oven and transfer it to a dry, heat-resistant surface. Let the pizza stand for 1 minute. Scatter the pizza with the basil, drizzle with the extra-virgin olive oil, slice, and serve.

MAKES ONE 12-INCH PIZZA; SERVES 2–4

This classic pizza features the colors of the Italian flag. It was created in the late nineteenth century and named for Italy's Queen Margherita.

Pizza with Pesto, Cherry Tomatoes & Mozzarella

Place a rack in the center of the oven and preheat to 450°F.

Place the dough ball on a lightly floured work surface. Coat your fingers with olive oil and press the dough from the center outward into a 12-inch round with a slightly raised edge (see page 15). If the dough springs back, cover it with a clean kitchen towel and let it rest for a few minutes, then continue. Cover the finished dough round with a clean kitchen towel and let rise for 15 minutes.

Carefully transfer the dough round to the pizza stone. Brush the raised edge of the dough with a light coating of olive oil. Spread the dough evenly with the pesto, leaving a ½-inch border uncovered. Scatter the tomatoes over the pesto, top with the mozzarella, and season generously with salt and pepper. Transfer the pizza stone to the oven. Bake until the crust is golden brown and the cheese is bubbling, 18–20 minutes.

Using oven mitts, carefully remove the pizza stone from the oven and transfer it to a dry, heat-resistant surface. Let stand for 1 minute, and then slice and serve.

MAKES ONE 12-INCH PIZZA; SERVES 2–4

1 ball Pizza Dough (page 20) or Whole-Wheat Pizza Dough (page 23), at room temperature

All-purpose flour for dusting

Olive oil for shaping and brushing

½ cup Basil Pesto (page 29)

6 oz cherry tomatoes, halved if large, left whole if small

¼ lb fresh mozzarella, sliced and then torn into bite-sized pieces

Salt and freshly ground pepper

This pizza is another take on the classic trio of Italian flavors: sweet tomatoes, fragrant basil, and creamy mozzarella cheese. Using cherry tomatoes of different colors makes a pizza that's a feast for the eyes as well as the taste buds.

Pizza with Eggplant, Roasted Peppers & Fontina

1 small eggplant (about 1 lb), sliced crosswise about ³⁄₈ inch thick

½ large white or yellow onion, thinly sliced

¼ cup olive oil, plus extra for shaping and brushing

Coarse salt

1 ball Pizza Dough (page 20), or Whole-Wheat Pizza Dough (page 23), at room temperature

All-purpose flour for dusting

Marinated Roasted Peppers (page 31)

½ tsp dried oregano

Freshly ground pepper

5 oz Italian fontina cheese, thinly sliced and then torn into bite-sized pieces

1 tbsp capers, rinsed and drained

Place a rack in the center of the oven and preheat to 450°F.

In a bowl, combine the eggplant, onion, ¼ cup olive oil, and 1½ teaspoons coarse salt. Spread in an even layer on a rimmed baking sheet and place in the oven. Roast, turning the vegetables over about every 10 minutes, until the eggplant is tender and lightly golden, about 35 minutes.

Meanwhile, place the dough ball on a lightly floured work surface. Coat your fingers with olive oil and press the dough from the center outward into a 12-inch round with a slightly raised edge (see page 15). If the dough springs back, cover it with a clean kitchen towel and let it rest for a few minutes, then continue. Cover the finished dough round with a clean kitchen towel and let rise for 15 minutes.

Carefully transfer the dough round to the pizza stone. Brush the raised edge of the dough with a light coating of olive oil. Arrange the peppers on the dough, leaving a ½-inch border uncovered. Arrange the eggplant and onion on top of the peppers, and then sprinkle with the oregano and season to taste with pepper. Top with the fontina and capers. Transfer the pizza stone to the oven. Bake until the crust is golden brown and the cheese is bubbling, 18–20 minutes.

Using oven mitts, carefully remove the pizza stone from the oven and transfer it to a dry, heat-resistant surface. Let stand for 1 minute, and then slice and serve.

MAKES ONE 12-INCH PIZZA; SERVES 2–4

Tiny capers add big bursts of briny Mediterranean flavor to this pizza. Whether packed in salt or brine, capers should always be rinsed and drained before use.

White Pizza with Garlic

1 ball Pizza Dough (page 20) or Whole-Wheat Pizza Dough (page 23), at room temperature

All-purpose flour for dusting

Olive oil for shaping and brushing

½ cup whole-milk ricotta cheese

2 cloves garlic, minced

½ cup loosely packed fresh herbs, torn into small pieces

3 oz fresh mozzarella cheese, sliced and torn into bite-sized pieces

2 oz Parmesan cheese, shaved with a vegetable peeler

Salt and freshly ground pepper

Extra-virgin olive oil for drizzling

Place a rack in the center of the oven and preheat to 450°F.

Place the dough ball on a lightly floured work surface. Coat your fingers with olive oil and press the dough from the center outward into a 12-inch round with a slightly raised edge (see page 15). If the dough springs back, cover it with a clean kitchen towel and let it rest for a few minutes, then continue. Cover the finished dough round with a clean kitchen towel and let rise for 15 minutes.

Meanwhile, in a bowl, whisk together the ricotta and garlic.

Carefully transfer the dough round to the pizza stone. Brush the raised edge of the dough with a light coating of olive oil. Spread the dough evenly with the ricotta mixture, leaving a ½-inch border uncovered. Sprinkle with one-half of the herbs. Top with the mozzarella and Parmesan and season generously with salt and pepper. Transfer the pizza stone to the oven. Bake until the crust is golden brown and the cheese is bubbling, 18–20 minutes.

Using oven mitts, carefully remove the pizza stone from the oven and transfer it to a dry, heat-resistant surface. Let stand for 2 minutes, and then sprinkle the pizza with the remaining herbs and drizzle with extra-virgin olive oil. Slice and serve.

MAKES ONE 12-INCH PIZZA; SERVES 2–4

This pizza is so named because it is made without tomatoes and with only light-colored cheeses. You can use one or any combination of soft, leafy herbs here. Choose from basil, parsley, chervil, tarragon, and oregano. (Use oregano very sparingly.)

Four-Cheese Pizza

Place a rack in the center of the oven and preheat to 450°F.

Place the dough ball on a lightly floured work surface. Coat your fingers with olive oil and press the dough from the center outward into a 12-inch round with a slightly raised edge (see page 15). If the dough springs back, cover it with a clean kitchen towel and let it rest for a few minutes, then continue. Cover the finished dough round with a clean kitchen towel and let rise for 15 minutes.

Carefully transfer the dough round to the pizza stone. Brush the raised edge of the dough with a light coating of olive oil. Spread the dough evenly with the tomato sauce, leaving a 1/2-inch border uncovered. Scatter the basil and arrange the prosciutto, if using, over the sauce. Top with the fresh and smoked mozzarella and the fontina. Season lightly with salt and pepper and sprinkle with the Parmesan. Transfer the pizza stone to the oven. Bake until the crust is golden brown and the cheese is bubbling, 18–20 minutes.

Using oven mitts, carefully remove the pizza stone from the oven and transfer it to a dry, heat-resistant surface. Let stand for 1 minute, and then slice and serve.

MAKES ONE 12-INCH PIZZA; SERVES 2–4

This classic pie is known as quattro formaggi in Italian. Be sure to use Italian fontina, a lovely smooth-melting cheese, rather than the domestic or Danish variety.

1 ball Pizza Dough (page 20) or Whole-Wheat Pizza Dough (page 23), at room temperature

All-purpose flour for dusting

Olive oil for shaping and brushing

1/2 cup Simple Tomato Sauce (page 24)

1/3 cup fresh basil leaves, torn into small pieces

1 thin slice prosciutto, fat removed and torn into small pieces (optional)

2 oz fresh mozzarella cheese, diced or sliced and torn into bite-sized pieces

2 oz smoked mozzarella cheese, shredded

2 oz Italian fontina cheese, shredded

Salt and freshly ground pepper

1 oz Parmesan cheese, coarsely grated

Pizza with Sun-Dried Tomato Pesto, Arugula & Mozzarella

1 ball Pizza Dough (page 20) or Whole-Wheat Pizza Dough (page 23), at room temperature

All-purpose flour for dusting

Olive oil for shaping and brushing

1/2 cup Sun-Dried Tomato Pesto (page 27) or Simple Tomato Sauce (page 24)

1 cup baby arugula leaves

1/4 lb fresh mozzarella cheese, sliced and torn into bite-sized pieces

Salt and freshly ground pepper

1 oz Parmesan cheese, finely grated

3 thin slices prosciutto, torn into small pieces (optional)

Place a rack in the center of the oven and preheat to 450°F.

Place the dough ball on a lightly floured work surface. Coat your fingers with olive oil and press the dough from the center outward into a 12-inch round with a slightly raised edge (see page 15). If the dough springs back, cover it with a clean kitchen towel and let it rest for a few minutes, then continue. Cover the finished dough round with a clean kitchen towel and let rise for 15 minutes.

Carefully transfer the dough round to the pizza stone. Brush the raised edge of the dough with a light coating of olive oil. Spread the dough evenly with the sun-dried tomato pesto, leaving a 1/2-inch border uncovered. Scatter with one-half of the arugula and top with the mozzarella. Season generously with salt and pepper and sprinkle with the Parmesan. Transfer the pizza stone to the oven. Bake until the crust is golden brown and the cheese is bubbling, 18–20 minutes.

Using oven mitts, carefully remove the pizza stone from the oven and transfer it to a dry, heat-resistant surface. Let stand for 1 minute, then scatter with the remaining arugula leaves and the prosciutto, if using. Slice and serve.

MAKES ONE 12-INCH PIZZA; SERVES 2–4

Packed with the one-two punch of sweet sun-dried tomato pesto and peppery arugula, this is a bold-flavored pie with modern-day sensibility. Use the optional prosciutto to add another layer of flavor, this one savory and salty.

Pizza with Salami, Fennel & Asiago Cheese

2 tbsp olive oil, plus extra for shaping and brushing

1 small fennel bulb, quartered, cored, and thinly sliced crosswise

Salt

1 ball Pizza Dough (page 20) or Whole-Wheat Pizza Dough (page 23), at room temperature

All-purpose flour for dusting

¾ cup Simple Tomato Sauce (page 24)

2 oz Genoa-style salami or soppressata, sliced and torn into bite-sized pieces

2 oz Asiago cheese, sliced and torn into bite-sized pieces

Freshly ground pepper

Place a rack in the center of the oven and preheat to 450°F.

In a frying pan over low heat, warm the 2 tablespoons olive oil. Add the fennel and season lightly with salt. Cover and cook until softened, stirring only occasionally, about 14 minutes. Remove the lid and cook, stirring frequently now, until much of the liquid has evaporated and the fennel is tender and translucent, 5–10 minutes more. Be careful not to let it scorch.

Place the dough ball on a lightly floured work surface. Coat your fingers with olive oil and press the dough from the center outward into a 12-inch round with a slightly raised edge (see page 15). If the dough springs back, cover it with a clean kitchen towel and let it rest for a few minutes, then continue. Cover the finished dough round with a clean kitchen towel and let rise for 15 minutes.

Carefully transfer the dough round to the pizza stone. Brush the raised edge of the dough with a light coating of olive oil. Spread the dough evenly with the tomato sauce, leaving a ½-inch border uncovered. Scatter the fennel and salami over the sauce, and then top with the Asiago. Season to taste with pepper. Transfer the pizza stone to the oven. Bake until the crust is golden brown and the cheese is bubbling, 18–20 minutes.

Using oven mitts, carefully remove the pizza stone from the oven and transfer it to a dry, heat-resistant surface. Let stand for 1 minute, and then slice and serve.

MAKES ONE 12-INCH PIZZA; SERVES 2–4

The wispy, feathery fennel fronds can be chopped and sprinkled onto the finished pizza as a garnish.

Pizza with Prosciutto & Caramelized Onions

Place a rack in the center of the oven and preheat to 450°F.

Place the dough ball on a lightly floured work surface. Coat your fingers with olive oil and press the dough from the center outward into a 12-inch round with a slightly raised edge (see page 15). If the dough springs back, cover it with a clean kitchen towel and let it rest for a few minutes, then continue. Cover the finished dough round with a clean kitchen towel and let rise for 15 minutes.

Meanwhile, in a dry frying pan over medium heat, cook the prosciutto, stirring occasionally, until crisp, about 5 minutes. Drain on paper towels.

Carefully transfer the dough round to the pizza stone. Brush the raised edge of the dough with a light coating of olive oil. Spread the dough evenly with the caramelized onions, leaving a 1/2-inch border uncovered. Scatter the crisped prosciutto over the onions, dot with teaspoonfuls of the mascarpone, and season to taste with pepper. Transfer the pizza stone to the oven. Bake until the crust is golden brown, 18–20 minutes.

Using oven mitts, carefully remove the pizza stone from the oven and transfer it to a dry, heat-resistant surface. Let stand for 1 minute, and then slice and serve.

MAKES ONE 12-INCH PIZZA; SERVES 2–4

1 ball Pizza Dough (page 20) or Whole-Wheat Pizza Dough (page 23), at room temperature

All-purpose flour for dusting

Olive oil for shaping and brushing

3 oz thick-cut prosciutto, diced

Caramelized Onions (page 30)

1/3 cup mascarpone cheese

Freshly ground pepper

When shopping for ingredients for this pizza, ask at the deli counter for a slice of prosciutto about 1/4 inch thick, which you can then cut into perfect dice. Gorgonzola cheese would be a delicious substitute for the mascarpone.

Pepperoni Pizza

Place a rack in the center of the oven and preheat to 450°F.

Place the dough ball on a lightly floured work surface. Coat your fingers with olive oil and press the dough from the center outward into a 12-inch round with a slightly raised edge (see page 15). If the dough springs back, cover it with a clean kitchen towel and let it rest for a few minutes, then continue. Cover the finished dough round with a clean kitchen towel and let rise for 15 minutes.

Carefully transfer the dough round to the pizza stone. Brush the raised edge of the dough with a light coating of olive oil. Spread the dough evenly with the tomato sauce, leaving a ½-inch border uncovered. Sprinkle the oregano and mozzarella over the sauce, and then top with the pepperoni and pecorino romano. Season to taste with pepper. Transfer the pizza stone to the oven. Bake until the crust is golden brown and the cheese is bubbling, 18–20 minutes.

Using oven mitts, carefully remove the pizza stone from the oven and transfer it to a dry, heat-resistant surface. Let stand for 2 minutes, and then slice and serve.

MAKES ONE 12-INCH PIZZA; SERVES 2–4

1 ball Pizza Dough
(page 20) or Whole-Wheat
Pizza Dough (page 23),
at room temperature

All-purpose flour
for dusting

Olive oil for shaping
and brushing

¾ cup Simple Tomato
Sauce (page 24)

¼ tsp dried oregano

2 oz low-moisture
whole-milk mozzarella
cheese, shredded

2 oz thinly sliced pepperoni

2 oz pecorino romano or
Parmesan cheese, shaved
with a vegetable peeler

Freshly ground pepper

To render some of the fat from the pepperoni, cook the slices in a dry frying pan over medium heat for about 5 minutes; drain them briefly on paper towels before topping the pizza. This will also ensure that the pepperoni bakes up extra-crisp.

Four Seasons Pizza

1 ball Pizza Dough (page 20) or Whole-Wheat Pizza Dough (page 23), at room temperature

All-purpose flour for dusting

1 tbsp olive oil, plus extra for shaping and brushing

2 oz small cremini mushrooms, brushed clean and quartered

Salt

1 clove garlic, minced

1/2 cup Simple Tomato Sauce (page 24)

2 oz low-moisture whole-milk mozzarella cheese, shredded

1 oz thinly sliced prosciutto, torn into bite-sized pieces

1/2 cup marinated artichoke hearts, well-drained and slivered

1/4 cup Kalamata or Niçoise olives, pitted and halved

1 oz Parmesan cheese, coarsely grated

Freshly ground pepper

Place a rack in the center of the oven and preheat to 450°F.

Place the dough ball on a lightly floured work surface. Coat your fingers with olive oil and press the dough from the center outward into a 12-inch round with a slightly raised edge (see page 15). If the dough springs back, cover it with a clean kitchen towel and let it rest for a few minutes, then continue. Cover the finished dough round with a clean kitchen towel and let rise for 15 minutes.

Meanwhile, in a frying pan over medium heat, warm 1 tablespoon olive oil. Add the mushrooms and season lightly with salt. Cook, stirring frequently, until the mushrooms are softened and lightly golden, about 5 minutes. Stir in the garlic and cook for 30 seconds more.

Carefully transfer the dough round to the pizza stone. Brush the raised edge of the dough with a light coating of olive oil. Spread the dough evenly with the tomato sauce, leaving a 1/2-inch border uncovered. Scatter the mozzarella over the tomato sauce. Top one quadrant of dough with the mushrooms, a second with the prosciutto, a third with the artichoke hearts, and the last with the olives. Sprinkle the entire pizza with the Parmesan and season to taste with pepper. Transfer the pizza stone to the oven. Bake until the crust is golden brown and the cheese is bubbling, 18–20 minutes.

Using oven mitts, carefully remove the pizza stone from the oven and transfer it to a dry, heat-resistant surface. Let stand for 2 minutes, and then slice and serve.

MAKES ONE 12-INCH PIZZA; SERVES 2–4

Quattro stagione, or four seasons, pizza is ideal for serving two people. Slice the pie into eighths and serve a wedge of each "season."

Modern Pizzas

Jerk Chicken Pizza with Smoked Gouda & Red Onion

FOR THE JERK CHICKEN

½ small yellow onion, sliced

2 green onions, white and green parts, thickly sliced

1 tsp *each* ground allspice and dried thyme

½ tsp ground nutmeg

1 tbsp olive oil

1 habanero chile, stemmed and seeded

Salt

1 large skinless, boneless chicken breast half

1 ball Pizza Dough (page 20), at room temperature

All-purpose flour for dusting

Olive oil for shaping and brushing

Salt and freshly ground pepper

½ small red onion, thinly sliced

2 tbsp roughly chopped fresh cilantro leaves, plus cilantro leaves for garnish

¼ lb smoked Gouda cheese, shredded

To make the jerk chicken, in a food processor, combine the yellow onion, green onions, allspice, thyme, nutmeg, olive oil, and chile. Season to taste with salt. Process until smooth, about 20 seconds. Transfer the marinade to a baking dish, add the chicken breast, and turn to coat evenly. Cover and refrigerate for 1–4 hours.

Place a rack in the center of the oven and preheat to 450°F.

Place the dough ball on a lightly floured work surface. Coat your fingers with olive oil and press the dough from the center outward into a 12-inch round with a slightly raised edge (see page 15). If the dough springs back, cover it with a clean kitchen towel and let it rest for a few minutes, then continue. Cover the finished dough round with a clean kitchen towel and let rise for 15 minutes.

Meanwhile, grill, sauté, or broil the marinated chicken breast until well browned, firm, and opaque throughout, about 4 minutes on each side. Transfer to a cutting board and let stand for 5 minutes. Cut the chicken into ¾-inch pieces.

Carefully transfer the dough round to the pizza stone. Brush the raised edge of the dough with a light coating of olive oil. Season the dough generously with salt and pepper. Arrange the red onion over the dough, leaving a ½-inch border uncovered. Scatter the chopped cilantro on top and sprinkle with the Gouda. Transfer the pizza stone to the oven. Bake until the crust is golden brown and the cheese is bubbling, 18–20 minutes.

Using oven mitts, carefully remove the pizza stone from the oven and transfer it to a dry, heat-resistant surface. Let stand for 1 minute, and then top with the chicken and cilantro leaves. Slice and serve.

MAKES ONE 12-INCH PIZZA; SERVES 2–4

Pizza with Chicken & Basil Pesto

1 large skinless, boneless chicken breast half or rotisserie chicken breast half, skin removed and shredded

1 tbsp olive oil, plus extra for shaping and brushing

Salt and freshly ground pepper

1 ball Pizza Dough (page 20) or Whole-Wheat Pizza Dough (page 23), at room temperature

All-purpose flour for dusting

½ cup Basil Pesto (page 29)

2 oz Parmesan cheese, shaved with a vegetable peeler or coarsely grated

To reduce the pizza preparation time to virtually nothing, use rotisserie chicken and best-quality prepared basil pesto.

If you are using uncooked chicken, pound the chicken breast to an even $3/8$-inch thickness, and then brush with the 1 tablespoon olive oil and season to taste with salt and pepper. Grill, sauté, or broil the chicken breast for about 3 minutes on each side until just firm. Transfer to a cutting board and let stand for 5 minutes. Cut the chicken breast crosswise into $1/8$-inch slices. Don't worry if the chicken breast is still pink in the center; it will continue cooking in the oven. Set aside. (If you are using rotisserie chicken, you can skip this step.)

Place a rack in the center of the oven and preheat to 450°F.

Place the dough ball on a lightly floured work surface. Coat your fingers with olive oil and press the dough from the center outward into a 12-inch round with a slightly raised edge (see page 15). If the dough springs back, cover it with a clean kitchen towel and let it rest for a few minutes, then continue. Cover the finished dough round with a clean kitchen towel and let rise for 15 minutes.

Carefully transfer the dough round to the pizza stone. Brush the raised edge of the dough with a light coating of olive oil. Spread the dough evenly with the pesto, leaving a ½-inch border uncovered. Arrange the chicken slices over the pesto and top with the Parmesan. Transfer the pizza stone to the oven. Bake until the crust is golden brown and the cheese is bubbling, 18–20 minutes.

Using oven mitts, carefully remove the pizza stone from the oven and transfer it to a dry, heat-resistant surface. Let stand for 1 minute, and then slice and serve.

MAKES ONE 12-INCH PIZZA; SERVES 2–4

Pizza with Garlicky Shrimp & Cherry Tomatoes

Place a rack in the center of the oven and preheat to 450°F.

Place the dough ball on a lightly floured work surface. Coat your fingers with olive oil and press the dough from the center outward into a 12-inch round with a slightly raised edge (see page 15). If the dough springs back, cover it with a clean kitchen towel and let it rest for a few minutes, then continue. Cover the finished dough round with a clean kitchen towel and let rise for 15 minutes.

Meanwhile, in a bowl, combine the shrimp, garlic, oregano, and the 1 tablespoon olive oil. Toss to coat the shrimp.

Carefully transfer the dough round to the pizza stone. Brush the raised edge of the dough with a light coating of olive oil. Season the dough generously with salt and pepper. Scatter the shrimp and then the cherry tomatoes evenly over the dough, leaving a ½-inch border uncovered. Transfer the pizza stone to the oven. Bake until the crust is golden brown and the shrimp are pink, 16–18 minutes.

Using oven mitts, carefully remove the pizza stone from the oven and transfer it to a dry, heat-resistant surface. Garnish with the parsley, slice, and serve.

MAKES ONE 12-INCH PIZZA; SERVES 2–4

The high heat of the oven is enough to cook these little shrimp, so there is no need to pre-cook them. For the best flavor, choose fresh wild shrimp. Paired with a Caesar salad, this modern pizza makes a light and pleasing summer supper.

1 ball Pizza Dough (page 20) or Whole-Wheat Pizza Dough (page 23), at room temperature

All-purpose flour for dusting

1 tbsp olive oil, plus extra for shaping and brushing

½ lb small shrimp, peeled, deveined, and halved lengthwise

2 large cloves garlic, minced

½ tsp dried oregano

Salt and freshly ground pepper

1 cup cherry tomatoes, halved if large, left whole if small

⅓ cup fresh flat-leaf parsley leaves, coarsely chopped

Pizza with Shrimp & White Bean Purée

Place a rack in the center of the oven and preheat to 450°F.

Place the dough ball on a lightly floured work surface. Coat your fingers with olive oil and press the dough from the center outward into a 12-inch round with a slightly raised edge (see page 15). If the dough springs back, cover it with a clean kitchen towel and let it rest for a few minutes, then continue. Cover the finished dough round with a clean kitchen towel and let rise for 15 minutes.

Meanwhile, in a food processor, combine the white beans, garlic, ¼ teaspoon salt, pepper to taste, and 1½ tablespoons of the olive oil. Process until smooth, about 10 seconds. Set aside.

In a bowl, combine the shrimp, dried oregano, ¼ teaspoon salt, pepper to taste, and the remaining 1 tablespoon olive oil.

Carefully transfer the dough round to the pizza stone. Brush the raised edge of the dough with a light coating of olive oil. Season the dough generously with salt and pepper. Spread the white bean purée evenly over the dough, leaving a ½-inch border uncovered. Scatter the shrimp and garlicky bread crumbs, if using, over the purée. Transfer the pizza stone to the oven. Bake until the crust is golden brown and the shrimp are pink, 16–18 minutes.

Using oven mitts, carefully remove the pizza stone from the oven and transfer it to a dry, heat-resistant surface. Garnish with the fresh herbs, slice, and serve.

MAKES ONE 12-INCH PIZZA; SERVES 2–4

1 ball Pizza Dough (page 20) or Whole-Wheat Pizza Dough (page 23), at room temperature

All-purpose flour for dusting

2½ tbsp olive oil, plus extra for shaping and brushing

1 cup canned small white beans, rinsed and drained

1 small clove garlic, minced

Salt and freshly ground pepper

½ lb small shrimp, peeled, deveined, and halved lengthwise

¼ tsp dried oregano

2 tbsp Garlicky Bread Crumbs (see page 58; optional)

1 tbsp chopped fresh basil or flat-leaf parsley

2 tsp minced fresh oregano

Fresh Clam Pizza with Tomatoes & Bread Crumbs

FOR THE GARLICKY
BREAD CRUMBS

2 large cloves garlic

5 oz coarse country bread,
crusts removed and torn
into large pieces

Salt and freshly
ground pepper

2 tbsp olive oil

1 ball Pizza Dough
(page 20) or Whole-Wheat
Pizza Dough (page 23),
at room temperature

All-purpose flour
for dusting

Olive oil for shaping
and brushing

2½ lb littleneck or
Manila clams

Salt and freshly
ground pepper

1 large plum tomato,
thinly sliced

1½ tsp dried oregano

2 tbsp coarsely chopped
fresh flat-leaf parsley

To make the garlicky bread crumbs, in a food processor with the motor running, add the garlic and process until minced, about 10 seconds. Add the bread, ½ teaspoon salt, and pepper to taste and process until coarse crumbs form, 5–10 seconds. Add the olive oil and pulse until combined. Measure out ½ cup bread crumbs and set aside. (Extra bread crumbs can be frozen in an airtight container for up to 2 months; thaw for 5 minutes at room temperature before using.)

Place a rack in the center of the oven and preheat to 450°F.

Place the dough ball on a lightly floured work surface. Coat your fingers with olive oil and press the dough from the center outward into a 12-inch round with a slightly raised edge (see page 15). If the dough springs back, cover it with a clean kitchen towel and let it rest for a few minutes, then continue. Cover the finished dough round with a clean kitchen towel and let rise for 15 minutes.

Meanwhile, put the clams and ¼ cup water in a saucepan over medium heat, cover the pan, and cook until the clams open, 5–7 minutes. Discard any that do not open. Remove the meat from the shells (you should have about ½ cup) and let dry on paper towels.

Carefully transfer the dough round to the pizza stone. Brush the raised edge of the dough with a light coating of olive oil. Season the dough generously with salt and pepper. Arrange the tomato slices evenly on top, leaving a ½-inch border uncovered. Sprinkle the tomato slices with the oregano, scatter the clams on top, and then sprinkle with the ½ cup of bread crumbs. Transfer the pizza stone to the oven. Bake until the crust is golden brown, 16–18 minutes.

Using oven mitts, carefully remove the pizza stone from the oven and transfer it to a dry, heat-resistant surface. Garnish with the parsley, slice, and serve.

MAKES ONE 12-INCH PIZZA; SERVES 2–4

Pizza with Chorizo & Roasted Peppers

1 ball Pizza Dough (page 20) or Whole-Wheat Pizza Dough (page 23), at room temperature

All-purpose flour for dusting

Olive oil for shaping and brushing

Salt and freshly ground pepper

¼ lb Spanish dry-cured chorizo, thinly sliced

3 oz Manchego or pecorino romano cheese, shaved with a vegetable peeler

Marinated Roasted Peppers (page 31)

Place a rack in the center of the oven and preheat to 450°F.

Place the dough ball on a lightly floured work surface. Coat your fingers with olive oil and press the dough from the center outward into a 12-inch round with a slightly raised edge (see page 15). If the dough springs back, cover it with a clean kitchen towel and let it rest for a few minutes, then continue. Cover the finished dough round with a clean kitchen towel and let rise for 15 minutes.

Carefully transfer the dough round to the pizza stone. Brush the raised edge of the dough with a light coating of olive oil. Season the dough lightly with salt and pepper. Arrange the chorizo slices over the dough, leaving a ½-inch border uncovered. Top with the Manchego and the roasted peppers. Transfer the pizza stone to the oven. Bake until the crust is golden brown and the cheese is bubbling, 18–20 minutes.

Using oven mitts, carefully remove the pizza stone from the oven and transfer it to a dry, heat-resistant surface. Let stand for 1 minute, and then slice and serve.

MAKES ONE 12-INCH PIZZA; SERVES 2–4

Manchego is one of the gastronomic prides of Spain and is the most popular of all the Spanish cheeses. If it is unavailable, substitute a young pecorino romano. Be sure to use dry-cured Spanish chorizo on this pizza, not fresh Mexican chorizo.

Pizza with Potatoes & Pancetta

Place a rack in the center of the oven and preheat to 450°F.

Cut the potatoes into golf ball–sized pieces, if necessary. Place the potatoes in a saucepan, add water to cover by about 2 inches, and season generously with salt. Bring to a boil over high heat, and then reduce the heat and simmer until the potatoes are tender but not mushy, about 10 minutes. Drain and let cool slightly. Slice the potatoes ¼-inch thick. In a bowl, combine the potato slices, 2 teaspoons of the olive oil, the oregano, ¼ teaspoon salt, and pepper to taste. Toss to coat and set aside. Meanwhile, in a frying pan over medium-low heat, warm the remaining 1 teaspoon olive oil. Add the pancetta and sauté until crisp, about 4 minutes.

Place the dough ball on a lightly floured work surface. Coat your fingers with olive oil and press the dough from the center outward into a 12-inch round with a slightly raised edge (see page 15). If the dough springs back, cover it with a clean kitchen towel and let it rest for a few minutes, then continue. Cover the finished dough round with a clean kitchen towel and let rise for 15 minutes.

Carefully transfer the dough round to the pizza stone. Brush the raised edge of the dough with a light coating of olive oil. Season the dough lightly with salt and pepper. Arrange the potato slices on the dough, leaving a ½-inch border uncovered. Scatter the pancetta over the potatoes and top with the Taleggio. Transfer the pizza stone to the oven. Bake until the crust is golden brown and the cheese is bubbling, 18–20 minutes.

Using oven mitts, carefully remove the pizza stone from the oven and transfer it to a dry, heat-resistant surface. Let stand for 2 minutes, and then slice and serve.

MAKES ONE 12-INCH PIZZA; SERVES 2–4

8 oz small red potatoes

Salt

3 tsp olive oil, plus extra for shaping and brushing

¼ tsp dried oregano

Freshly ground pepper

3 oz pancetta, thickly sliced and then diced

1 ball Pizza Dough (page 20) or Whole-Wheat Pizza Dough (page 23), at room temperature

All-purpose flour for dusting

¼ lb Taleggio or Italian fontina cheese, cut into large cubes

Paired with rich cheese and robust flavors, sliced potatoes are an unusual—but hearty and delicious—topping for pizza.

Egg, Sausage & Cheese Breakfast Pizzas

All-purpose flour
for dusting

1 ball Semolina
Pizza Dough (page 21),
at room temperature

Olive oil for shaping
and brushing

6 oz sweet or hot Italian
sausage, casing removed

4 large eggs, at room
temperature

¾ cup Simple Tomato
Sauce (page 24; optional)

3 oz low-moisture
whole-milk mozzarella
cheese, shredded

Salt and freshly
ground pepper

1 tbsp chopped fresh chives

Try a new twist on breakfast by serving eggs, sausage, and cheese on top of a golden pizza round.

Place a rack in the center of the oven and preheat to 450°F.

On a lightly floured work surface, divide the dough into 4 equal balls. Coat your fingers with olive oil and press each ball of dough into a 5-inch round. Press down on the center of each round to create a well. Cover the dough rounds with a clean kitchen towel and let rise for 15 minutes.

Meanwhile, in a nonstick frying pan over medium heat, sauté the sausage, breaking it up into small pieces with a wooden spoon, until golden brown, about 6 minutes. Drain on paper towels and set aside. Break each of the eggs into a small ramekin or saucer and set aside.

Carefully transfer the dough rounds to the pizza stone. Dimple the center of each round firmly with your fingertips. Brush each round with a light coating of olive oil and spread evenly with 3 tablespoons tomato sauce, if using, leaving a ¼-inch border uncovered. Arrange the mozzarella and sausage over the tomato sauce, leaving a space in the center for an egg. Season lightly with salt and pepper. Transfer the pizza stone to the oven. Bake for about 12 minutes. Open the oven door. Without pulling out the oven rack, if possible, use the back of a wooden spoon to press down on the center of each pizza, and then quickly and carefully slide 1 egg onto the center of each pizza. Bake until the egg whites are set and the yolks are still runny, 4–5 minutes more.

Using oven mitts, carefully remove the pizza stone from the oven and transfer it to a dry, heat-resistant surface. Let the pizzas stand for 1 minute, sprinkle with the chives, and serve.

MAKES FOUR 5-INCH PIZZAS; SERVES 4

Pizza with Artichokes, Red Onion & Tapenade

4 baby artichokes, tough outer leaves removed, stems trimmed and peeled

Juice of 1 lemon

Salt

2 tbsp olive oil, plus extra for shaping and brushing

1 small red onion, thinly sliced and separated into rings

1 ball Pizza Dough (page 20) or Whole-Wheat Pizza Dough (page 23), at room temperature

All-purpose flour for dusting

½ cup Black Olive Tapenade (page 26)

3 oz fresh goat cheese or fresh mozzarella, crumbled or cut into 1-inch pieces

½ cup Garlicky Bread Crumbs (see page 58; optional)

Toss the artichokes with the lemon juice. Fill a saucepan three-fourths full with water, bring to a boil over high heat, and season moderately with salt. Drop in the artichokes and cook until the bases are tender when pierced with a sharp knife, about 7 minutes. Drain and let cool. Cut into quarters and set aside.

In a frying pan over medium heat, warm the 2 tablespoons olive oil. Add the onion and 2 tablespoons water and cook, stirring occasionally, until all the liquid has evaporated, 7–8 minutes. Reduce the heat and cook until the onion is softened and lightly browned, 15–20 minutes.

Place a rack in the center of the oven and preheat to 450°F.

Place the dough ball on a lightly floured work surface. Coat your fingers with olive oil and press the dough from the center outward into a 12-inch round with a slightly raised edge (see page 15). If the dough springs back, cover it with a clean kitchen towel and let it rest for a few minutes, then continue. Cover the finished dough round with a clean kitchen towel and let rise for 15 minutes.

Carefully transfer the dough round to the pizza stone. Brush the raised edge of the dough with a light coating of olive oil. Spread the dough evenly with the tapenade, leaving a ½-inch border uncovered. Spoon the onions and artichokes over the tapenade and top with the goat cheese. Sprinkle with the bread crumbs, if using. Transfer the pizza stone to the oven. Bake until the crust is golden brown, 18–20 minutes.

Using oven mitts, carefully remove the pizza stone from the oven and transfer it to a dry, heat-resistant surface. Let stand for 1 minute, and then slice and serve.

MAKES ONE 12-INCH PIZZA; SERVES 2–4

Pizza with Coppa, Soppressata & Prosciutto

Place a rack in the center of the oven and preheat to 450°F.

Place the dough ball on a lightly floured work surface. Coat your fingers with olive oil and press the dough from the center outward into a 12-inch round with a slightly raised edge (see page 15). If the dough springs back, cover it with a clean kitchen towel and let it rest for a few minutes, then continue. Cover the finished dough round with a clean kitchen towel and let rise for 15 minutes.

Carefully transfer the dough round to the pizza stone. Brush the raised edge of the dough with a light coating of olive oil. Spread the dough evenly with the tomato sauce, leaving a ½-inch border uncovered. Layer on the coppa, soppressata, and prosciutto, and then top with the pecorino romano shavings. Season to taste with pepper. Transfer the pizza stone to the oven. Bake until the crust is golden brown, 9–12 minutes.

Using oven mitts, carefully remove the pizza stone from the oven and transfer it to a dry, heat-resistant surface. Let stand for 1 minute, and then slice and serve.

MAKES ONE 12-INCH PIZZA; SERVES 2–4

This pizza features a savory trio of salumi, or Italian cured meats. You can shuffle the flavors and textures by substituting bresaola (air-dried beef) for the coppa and any other best-quality salami for the soppressata.

1 ball Pizza Dough (page 20) or Whole-Wheat Pizza Dough (page 23), at room temperature

All-purpose flour for dusting

Olive oil for shaping and brushing

¾ cup Simple Tomato Sauce (page 24)

1 oz coppa, thinly sliced and then torn into bite-sized pieces

1 oz soppressata, thinly sliced and then torn into bite-sized pieces

1 oz prosciutto, thinly sliced and then torn into bite-sized pieces

2 oz pecorino romano or Parmesan cheese, shaved with a vegetable peeler

Freshly ground pepper

Meatball Pizza

To make the meatballs, place the bread in a bowl and cover with ⅓ cup warm water. Let stand for 10 minutes, turning to moisten evenly. Squeeze gently to remove some of the water and then tear the bread into 1-inch chunks. Add the veal, sausage, garlic, parsley, egg white, half of the Parmesan, ¼ teaspoon salt, and pepper to taste. Mix thoroughly with moistened hands. Form the meat mixture into 10 balls. Place the meatballs on a parchment paper–lined rimmed baking sheet, cover with plastic wrap, and chill for at least 2 hours or up to overnight.

Place a rack in the center of the oven and preheat to 450°F.

Place the pan of meatballs in the oven and cook until golden brown, about 15 minutes. Let cool and then cut each meatball in half. Meanwhile, in a frying pan over medium heat, warm the 1 tablespoon olive oil. Add the onion and season lightly with salt. Sauté until softened, about 8 minutes.

Place the dough ball on a lightly floured work surface. Coat your fingers with olive oil and press the dough from the center outward into a 12-inch round with a slightly raised edge (see page 15). If the dough springs back, cover it with a clean kitchen towel and let it rest for a few minutes, then continue. Cover the finished dough round with a clean kitchen towel and let rise for 15 minutes.

Carefully transfer the dough round to the pizza stone. Brush the raised edge of the dough with a light coating of olive oil. Spread the dough with the tomato sauce, leaving a ½-inch border uncovered. Scatter the onion over the sauce. Arrange the halved meatballs on top. Sprinkle with the mozzarella and season to taste with pepper. Transfer the pizza stone to the oven. Bake until the crust is golden brown and the cheese is bubbling, 18–20 minutes.

Using oven mitts, carefully remove the pizza stone from the oven and transfer it to a dry, heat-resistant surface. Let stand for 2 minutes, sprinkle with the remaining Parmesan, and then slice and serve.

MAKES ONE 12-INCH PIZZA; SERVES 2–4

1 large slice stale white bread, crusts removed

4 oz ground veal or beef, very cold

3 oz sweet or hot Italian sausage, very cold, casing removed

1 small clove garlic, minced

1 tbsp minced fresh flat-leaf parsley

1 large egg white, lightly beaten

2 oz Parmesan cheese, finely grated

Salt and freshly ground pepper

1 tbsp olive oil, plus extra for shaping and brushing

1 small yellow onion, diced

1 ball Semolina Pizza Dough (page 21), at room temperature

All-purpose flour for dusting

¾ cup Simple Tomato Sauce (page 24)

¼ lb low-moisture whole-milk mozzarella cheese, shredded

Sausage & Artichoke Calzone

½ lb sweet or hot Italian sausage, casing removed

1 large egg

1 tbsp milk

All-purpose flour for dusting

1 ball Pizza Dough (page 20), at room temperature

Salt and freshly ground pepper

1 jar (6½ oz) marinated artichoke hearts, drained and cut into bite-sized pieces

1 oz Parmesan cheese, finely grated, plus 1 tbsp for sprinkling

2 oz Italian fontina or smoked mozzarella cheese, shredded

6–8 fresh basil leaves, torn into small pieces

½ cup Simple Tomato Sauce (page 24; optional), warmed or at room temperature

Place a rack in the center of the oven and preheat to 450°F.

In a frying pan over medium-low heat, sauté the sausage, breaking it up into small pieces with a spoon, until no trace of pink remains, 5–7 minutes. Drain on paper towels and set aside. In a bowl, lightly beat together the egg and milk.

On a lightly floured work surface, divide the dough in half and shape each half into a ball. Cover the one dough ball with a clean kitchen towel and set aside. Dust the top of the other dough ball with flour and, using a rolling pin, roll out to a 7-inch round of even thickness. Repeat with the second ball of dough. Cover both rounds with a clean kitchen towel and let rise for 5 minutes.

Season the dough rounds lightly with salt and pepper. Spoon one-half of the artichokes over one half of a dough round, leaving a ¾-inch border uncovered. Top with one-half each of the cooked sausage, 1 oz Parmesan, fontina, and basil. Make sure the filling isn't mounded too high in the center; it should evenly cover half of the dough round. Gently fold the uncovered half over to enclose the filling. Firmly pinch and crimp the edges to seal. Repeat with the second dough round.

Carefully transfer the filled calzones to the pizza stone. Brush the tops with the egg mixture and sprinkle each with ½ tablespoon of the remaining Parmesan. Cut a small steam vent in the top of each calzone. Transfer the pizza stone to the oven. Bake until golden brown, 20–25 minutes.

Using oven mitts, carefully remove the pizza stone from the oven and transfer it to a dry, heat-resistant surface. Let stand for 15–20 minutes, then cut into halves and serve warm. If desired, serve the tomato sauce on the side.

MAKES 2 CALZONES; SERVES 2

Broccoli & Cheese Stromboli

Place a rack in the center of the oven and preheat to 400°F.

Fill a saucepan three-fourths full with water, bring to a boil over high heat, and season generously with salt. Drop in the broccoli florets and cook until crisp-tender, 2–3 minutes. Drain and let cool, then coarsely chop. In a bowl, combine the ricotta, provolone, and basil, and mix well.

Place the dough ball on a lightly floured work surface. Dust the top of the dough with flour and, using a rolling pin, roll out to a 9-by-12-inch rectangle of even thickness. If the dough springs back, let it rest, uncovered, for a few minutes, then continue. (It will take persistence to coax the dough into a rectangle.) Cover the finished dough rectangle with a clean kitchen towel and let rise for 10 minutes.

Carefully transfer the dough rectangle to the pizza stone. With the long side of the dough facing you, spread the cheese mixture evenly over the dough, leaving a 1-inch border uncovered on all sides. Scatter the broccoli evenly over the cheese and season generously with salt and pepper. Starting with the long edge nearest you, gently roll up the dough, lightly compressing the filling. Crimp firmly to seal, but avoid pressing down too hard. Turn the stuffed roll seam side down, cover with a clean kitchen towel, and let rise for 5 minutes. Brush the roll lightly with olive oil, cut a few small steam vents in the top, and sprinkle with coarse sea salt. Transfer the pizza stone to the oven. Bake until golden brown, about 35–40 minutes.

Using oven mitts, carefully remove the pizza stone from the oven and transfer it to a dry, heat-resistant surface. Let the stromboli stand for 15–20 minutes and then use a serrated knife to slice it crosswise into rounds. If desired, serve the tomato sauce on the side.

MAKES ONE 12-INCH STUFFED ROLL; SERVES 4–6

Table salt

1 1/2 cups broccoli florets

2/3 cup whole-milk ricotta cheese

2 oz sliced provolone cheese, torn into small pieces

2 tbsp coarsely chopped fresh basil leaves

1 ball Pizza Dough (page 20), at room temperature

All-purpose flour for dusting

Freshly ground pepper

Olive oil for brushing

Coarse sea salt for sprinkling

1 cup Simple Tomato Sauce (page 24; optional), warmed or at room temperature

For an impressive presentation, you can make the stromboli into a pizza ring. Double the recipe (including the amount of dough), and, after stuffing the roll, attach the ends to form a ring. Increase the cooking time by about 15 minutes.

Fig & Mascarpone Pizza

6 tbsp balsamic vinegar

1 ball Pizza Dough
(page 20) or Whole-Wheat
Pizza Dough (page 23),
at room temperature

All-purpose flour
for dusting

Olive oil for shaping

2 tsp walnut oil

1 tsp sugar

1/4 tsp ground nutmeg

1/2 cup mascarpone cheese

6–8 ripe figs,
quartered lengthwise

*This stunning pizza
will impress with both
its beauty and its
luscious, summery
flavor. Serve it as
an appetizer or
as a light dessert.*

Place a rack in the center of the oven and preheat to 450°F.

In a small saucepan over medium heat, simmer the balsamic vinegar until syrupy and reduced to 2 tablespoons, 4–8 minutes. Set aside.

Place the dough ball on a lightly floured surface. Coat your fingers with olive oil and press the dough from the center outward into a 12-inch round with a slightly raised edge (see page 15). If the dough springs back, cover it with a clean kitchen towel and let it rest for a few minutes, then continue. Cover the finished dough round with a clean kitchen towel and let rise for 15 minutes.

Carefully transfer the dough round to the pizza stone. Brush with the walnut oil. With a fork, prick the surface of the dough several times. Sprinkle the dough evenly with the sugar and nutmeg. Transfer the pizza stone to the oven. Bake until the crust is golden brown, 18–20 minutes. (Watch the pizza as it bakes and, using the back of a spoon, flatten any bubbles that form.)

Using oven mitts, carefully remove the pizza stone from the oven and transfer it to a dry, heat-resistant surface. Let the pizza stand until just warm, 10–15 minutes, then spread evenly with the mascarpone, leaving a 1/2-inch border uncovered. Scatter with the figs and drizzle with the balsamic syrup. (If the syrup is too thick to drizzle, re-warm it slightly.) Slice and serve.

MAKES ONE 12-INCH PIZZA; SERVES 4–6

New Ideas for the Pizza Stone

Focaccia

4½–5 cups
all-purpose flour

2 packages (5 tsp)
active dry yeast

2 tsp fine sea salt

1 tsp sugar

1¾ cups warm water
(110°F)

½ cup olive oil, plus extra
for greasing and brushing

1 tsp coarse sea salt
for topping (optional)

Chopped fresh rosemary
or oregano for topping
(optional)

In a food processor, combine 4½ cups flour, the yeast, fine sea salt, and sugar and pulse to blend. With the motor running, add the warm water and olive oil in a steady stream, and then pulse until the dough comes together, about 15 seconds. The dough should be tacky to the touch but not sticky. If the dough is too sticky, add up to ½ cup more flour. Place the dough in a large oiled bowl, turn to coat with oil, and cover with plastic wrap. Let the dough rise in a warm place until doubled in bulk, about 1¼ hours.

Turn the dough out onto a lightly floured work surface, punch it down, and pat and stretch the dough into a 15-inch square. If the dough springs back, cover it with a clean kitchen towel and let it rest for a few minutes, then continue. Carefully transfer the finished dough square to the pizza stone. Cover with a clean kitchen towel and let rise again for 1 hour.

Place a rack in the center of the oven and preheat to 400°F.

Dimple the dough by pressing your fingertips into it at 1-inch intervals over the entire surface, and then brush the surface of the dough generously with olive oil. Sprinkle with the coarse salt and herbs, if using. Transfer the pizza stone to the oven and bake the focaccia until golden brown, 20–30 minutes.

Using oven mitts, carefully remove the pizza stone from the oven and transfer it to a dry, heat-resistant surface. Cut into wedges or squares and serve.

MAKES 1 LARGE FLATBREAD

Focaccia is an all-purpose flatbread that can be toasted for breakfast, split in half and used for sandwiches for lunch, or tucked into a bread basket on the dinner table. A generous brushing of olive oil and large flakes of sea salt yield satisfying flavor.

Orange-Zest Scones

Place a rack in the center of the oven and preheat to 400°F.

In a food processor, combine the flour, brown sugar, baking powder, baking soda, salt, and orange zest and pulse to mix the ingredients. Add the butter and pulse just until the mixture is the consistency of coarse meal, 4 or 5 times. Then, add the milk, egg, and orange juice and process just until the mixture holds together, about 20 seconds.

Turn the dough out onto a lightly floured work surface and gently knead into a ball. Using a floured rolling pin, roll out the dough to about ¼ to ½-inch thick. Flour a 3-inch round biscuit cutter and use it to cut out as many rounds as possible. Transfer the rounds to the pizza stone, spacing them about 1 inch apart. Gather the scraps, roll out again, and cut more rounds. Brush the tops with milk and sprinkle with the coarse sugar. Transfer the pizza stone to the oven and bake until the scones are golden brown, about 15 minutes.

Using oven mitts, carefully remove the pizza stone from the oven and transfer it to a dry, heat-resistant surface. Transfer the scones to a wire rack, let cool briefly, and serve warm.

MAKES ABOUT 12 SCONES

2½ cups all-purpose flour, plus extra for dusting

½ cup firmly packed light brown sugar

2 tsp baking powder

1 tsp baking soda

1 tsp salt

¼ cup coarsely grated orange zest

6 tbsp cold unsalted butter, cut into ½-inch pieces

½ cup plus 1 tbsp whole milk, plus extra for brushing

1 large egg, lightly beaten

3 tbsp fresh orange juice

1 tbsp coarse sugar

Orange zest lends its tangy flavor to these simple scones. Serve them with fruit jam or lemon curd for a delightful breakfast or afternoon snack. You can also cut the scones into triangles (you won't have to worry about re-rolling scraps).

Baking Powder Biscuits

2 cups all-purpose flour,
plus extra for dusting

2$\frac{1}{2}$ tsp baking powder

$\frac{1}{2}$ tsp salt

6 tbsp cold unsalted butter,
cut into $\frac{1}{2}$-inch pieces

$\frac{3}{4}$ cup whole milk

*To make tender,
flaky biscuits, use
a light touch. For
buttermilk biscuits,
replace the milk with
buttermilk, reduce
the baking powder
to 2 teaspoons, and
add $\frac{1}{2}$ teaspoon
baking soda.*

Place a rack in the center of the oven and preheat to 425°F.

In a food processor, combine the flour, baking powder, and salt and pulse to mix the ingredients. Add the butter and pulse 3–4 times or just until the mixture forms large, coarse crumbs the size of small peas. Pour in the milk and pulse for a few seconds just until the dry ingredients are moistened.

Turn the dough out onto a lightly floured work surface and knead gently a few times until it clings together. Using a floured rolling pin, roll out the dough to about $\frac{3}{4}$ inch thick. Flour a 3-inch round biscuit cutter and use it to cut out as many rounds as possible. Transfer the rounds to the pizza stone, spacing them about 1 inch apart. Gather the scraps, roll out again, and cut more rounds. Transfer the pizza stone to the oven and bake until the biscuits are lightly browned, 15–18 minutes.

Using oven mitts, carefully remove the pizza stone from the oven and transfer it to a dry, heat-resistant surface. Transfer the biscuits to a wire rack, let cool briefly, and serve warm.

MAKES ABOUT 10 BISCUITS

Cheese Twists

Place a rack in the center of the oven and preheat to 425°F.

Place the dough ball on a lightly floured work surface. Dust the top of the dough with flour and, using a rolling pin, roll out to a 14-inch square of even thickness. If the dough springs back, let it rest, uncovered, for a few minutes, then continue. Cover the finished dough square with a clean kitchen towel and let rise for 10 minutes.

Brush the half of the dough farthest from you with olive oil, and sprinkle half of the Parmesan over the oil-brushed surface. Season with salt and pepper. Fold the uncovered half of the dough up over the cheese and press the edges to seal. Brush the dough with more oil and sprinkle with the remaining Parmesan.

Cut the dough crosswise into strips 1 inch wide. Pick up each strip and twist the ends in opposite directions 4 or 5 times to make a spiral. Place the strips on the pizza stone; be sure that at least two-thirds of the stone is covered. Transfer the pizza stone to the oven. Bake until the twists are golden brown and the cheese is bubbling, 15–18 minutes.

Using oven mitts, carefully remove the pizza stone from the oven and transfer it to a dry, heat-resistant surface. Transfer the cheese twists to a wire rack and let cool completely before serving.

MAKES ABOUT 14 CHEESE TWISTS

1 ball Pizza Dough (page 20), at room temperature

All-purpose flour for dusting

Olive oil for brushing

2/3 cup coarsely grated Parmesan cheese

Coarse salt and freshly ground pepper

This is a great way to use up any extra pizza dough you might have in the freezer. Use a top-quality Parmesan such as Parmigiano-Reggiano for these savory twists. To make garlicky cheese twists, sprinkle 1 clove garlic, minced, over the dough when you add the cheese.

Roasted Vegetables with Feta Cheese

1 small eggplant, about ¾ lb, trimmed and cut lengthwise into thin slices

1 zucchini, about ½ lb, trimmed and cut lengthwise into thin slices

1 yellow onion, cut crosswise into thin slices

1 large tomato or 2 plum tomatoes, cut crosswise into thin slices

3 tbsp olive oil

Coarse salt and freshly ground pepper

1 large clove garlic, chopped

1 tbsp chopped fresh oregano

½ cup crumbled feta cheese

1 tbsp red wine vinegar

¼ cup roughly chopped fresh basil or mint leaves (optional)

Place a rack in the center of the oven and preheat to 425°F.

Arrange the eggplant, zucchini, onion, and tomato slices in a single layer on the pizza stone. Brush with half of the olive oil. Turn the slices and brush with the remaining oil. Season generously with salt and pepper and sprinkle evenly with the garlic and oregano. Transfer the pizza stone to the oven and roast the vegetables, turning once, until tender when pierced with a fork and tinged with brown, 12–15 minutes. Using oven mitts, carefully remove the pizza stone from the oven and transfer it to a dry, heat-resistant surface. Sprinkle the tops of the vegetables with the feta. Return the pizza stone to the oven and continue to roast until the cheese is softened, 2–3 minutes.

Using oven mitts, carefully remove the pizza stone from the oven and transfer it to a dry, heat-resistant surface. Sprinkle the vegetables with the vinegar and basil, if using, and serve.

MAKES 4 SERVINGS

Use just about any vegetable medley you like for this simple yet flavorful dish. Serve as an accompaniment to meat or fish, or chop and add to pastas, salads, or pizzas.

Baked Chicken Strips

Place a rack in the center of the oven and preheat to 450°F.

Ready 3 shallow bowls or pie pans for coating the chicken: In the first bowl, stir together the flour, 1 teaspoon salt, and ¼ teaspoon pepper. In the second bowl, whisk the eggs. In the third bowl, spread out the panko.

Working with 1 piece at a time, dip the chicken into the flour, coating it completely and shaking off the excess; then into the egg, allowing the excess to drip off; and finally into the panko, again shaking off the excess. Lay the coated chicken pieces on the pizza stone. Transfer the pizza stone to the oven and bake until crisp and golden brown, about 30 minutes.

Using oven mitts, carefully remove the pizza stone from the oven and transfer it to a dry, heat-resistant surface. Serve the chicken strips with barbecue sauce or ketchup.

MAKES 4 SERVINGS

2 cups all-purpose flour

Salt and freshly ground pepper

2 large eggs

4 cups panko bread crumbs

4 boneless, skinless chicken breasts, cut into strips 1 inch wide

Barbecue sauce or ketchup for serving

Stuffed Mushrooms

8 portobello mushrooms,
brushed clean and
stemmed

6 tbsp olive oil,
plus extra if needed

6 cloves garlic, chopped

2 cups fresh flat-leaf
parsley leaves

Salt and freshly
ground pepper

8 thin slices prosciutto,
chopped (optional)

⅔ cup coarse fresh
bread crumbs

1⅓ cups grated
Parmesan cheese

Place a rack in the center of the oven and preheat to 375°F.

Rub the mushroom caps with 2 tablespoons of the olive oil and arrange on the pizza stone, gill side up.

In a blender or food processor, combine the remaining 4 tablespoons olive oil, the garlic, parsley, ½ teaspoon salt, and ½ teaspoon pepper and process until smooth. If the mixture seems too thick, add more olive oil a few drops at a time.

Spread the parsley mixture over the mushrooms, dividing it evenly and covering the gills all the way to the edges. If using prosciutto, divide it evenly among the mushrooms. Top with the bread crumbs and Parmesan. Transfer the pizza stone to the oven and bake until the mushrooms are juicy and tender when pricked with a fork, about 20 minutes.

Using oven mitts, carefully remove the pizza stone from the oven and transfer it to a dry, heat-resistant surface. Let cool slightly before serving.

MAKES 8 STUFFED MUSHROOMS

Flaky Apple Turnovers

Line a half-sheet pan or rimless baking sheet with wax paper. On a floured work surface, roll out the pastry dough into a 9-by-18-inch rectangle. Cut in half lengthwise, and then cut each half crosswise into 4 squares, for a total of 8 squares. Place the squares on the prepared pan, cover with wax paper, and refrigerate while preparing the filling.

To make the filling, in a large frying pan over medium-high heat, melt the butter. Add the apples and sauté until tender, 5–7 minutes. Sprinkle with the granulated sugar and lemon juice and sauté, stirring, for 1–2 minutes longer. Remove from the heat and let cool.

Remove the chilled puff pastry squares from the refrigerator and spread out on a clean work surface. Using a pastry brush, brush the surface of each square with some of the egg mixture, leaving a ¼-inch border around the edge. Place 2 tablespoons of the filling almost in the middle of each square, fold over to make a triangle, and press the edges together with the tines of a fork to seal. Place on the prepared baking sheet. Repeat with the remaining squares and filling. Cover with wax paper and refrigerate for 30 minutes.

Place a rack in the center of the oven and preheat to 425°F.

Transfer the pastries to the pizza stone. Brush the tops with the remaining egg mixture and sprinkle with the coarse sugar. Pierce the top of each pastry twice with the tines of a fork. Bake the turnovers for 20 minutes. Reduce the heat to 350°F and continue baking until golden brown and puffed, 15–20 minutes longer.

Using oven mitts, carefully remove the pizza stone from the oven and transfer it to a dry, heat-resistant surface. Transfer the turnovers to a wire rack and let cool for 15 minutes. Serve warm.

MAKES 8 TURNOVERS

All-purpose flour
for dusting

1 lb purchased puff pastry,
thawed if frozen

2 tbsp unsalted butter

4 large tart apples
such as Granny Smith or
pippin, about 1¾ lb total
weight, peeled, cored,
and thinly sliced

¼ cup granulated sugar

2 tsp fresh lemon juice

1 large egg, beaten with
1 tbsp whole milk

⅓ cup coarse sugar

These triangular pastries are the perfect size to eat out of hand. In the summertime, fresh berries, peaches, or nectarines can replace the apples. You will need about 4 cups fruit total.

Chocolate Chip Cookies

In a bowl, sift together the flour, baking soda, and salt; set aside. In a large bowl, combine the butter, brown sugar, and granulated sugar. Using a mixer on medium speed, beat until well blended, about 1 minute. Add the eggs and vanilla and beat on low speed until the eggs are completely incorporated, scraping down the bowl occasionally with a rubber spatula. Slowly add the flour mixture and beat on low speed just until incorporated. Add the chocolate chips and beat just until distributed.

On a lightly floured work surface, divide the dough in half. Shape each dough half into a log about 2 inches in diameter. Wrap the logs in plastic wrap and refrigerate until firm, at least 1 hour and up to 24 hours.

Place a rack in the center of the oven and preheat to 350°F.

Remove the dough logs from the refrigerator and cut into slices about ½ inch thick. Place the slices 3 inches apart on the pizza stone. (Refrigerate any remaining dough for up to 1 week or freeze for up to 1 month.) Transfer the pizza stone to the oven and bake until the cookie tops are lightly golden, 10–12 minutes.

Using oven mitts, carefully remove the pizza stone from the oven and transfer it to a dry, heat-resistant surface. Let the cookies cool on the stone for 5 minutes, then, using a wide metal spatula, transfer to wire racks to cool completely, about 30 minutes. Let the pizza stone cool completely before baking additional cookies.

MAKES DOUGH FOR ABOUT 32 COOKIES

---

2 cups all-purpose flour, plus extra for dusting

1 tsp baking soda

½ tsp salt

1 cup unsalted butter, at room temperature

¾ cup firmly packed light brown sugar

¾ cup granulated sugar

2 large eggs, cold

2 tsp pure vanilla extract

2 cups semisweet chocolate chips

Berry Galette

Homemade or purchased
pie dough for a 9-inch
single-crust pie, chilled

3 tbsp all-purpose flour,
plus extra for dusting

4 cups blackberries,
blueberries, or a mixture

2 tbsp lemon juice

3–4 tbsp sugar

1 large egg, beaten with
1 tbsp whole milk

Place a rack in the center of the oven and preheat to 425°F.

Place the dough on a lightly floured surface and roll out into a 13-inch round. Fold the round in half, transfer to the pizza stone, then unfold the round.

In a bowl, lightly toss together the berries, lemon juice, 2–3 tablespoons of the sugar (depending on the ripeness of the fruit), and the 3 tablespoons flour. Spoon the filling onto the dough, leaving a 2-inch border uncovered around the edge. Fold the edge up and over the filling, forming loose pleats all around the edge and leaving the center open. Brush the pleated dough with the egg mixture, then sprinkle it with the remaining 1 tablespoon sugar. You will not use all of the egg mixture. Transfer the pizza stone to the oven and bake until the filling is bubbling and the crust is golden brown, 30–35 minutes.

Using oven mitts, carefully remove the pizza stone from the oven and transfer it to a dry, heat-resistant surface. Let the galette cool slightly. Cut the galette into pie-shaped wedges to serve.

MAKES ONE 9-INCH GALETTE

This rustic, free-form pie is a gorgeous sight to behold, and it's fairly easy to make once you get the hang of pleating the dough around the filling. Nearly any fruit can stand in for the berries, such as strawberries, apples, peaches, or nectarines.

Index

weldon**owen**

415 Jackson Street, Suite 200, San Francisco, CA 94111
www.wopublishing.com

THE HAEGER NATURALSTONE™ PIZZA COOKBOOK
Conceived and produced by Weldon Owen Inc.
Copyright © 2011 Weldon Owen Inc.

Printed and bound by 1010 Printing, Ltd. in China
First printed in 2011
10 9 8 7 6 5 4 3 2 1

ISBN-13: 978-1-61628-261-5
ISBN-10: 1-61628-261-4

Weldon Owen is a division of
BONNIER

CREDITS
Photographs by David Matheson except the following:
front cover and pages 1; 35; 74–91 by Erin Kunkel
Food styling by Shelly Kaldunski except the following:
front cover and pages 1; 35; 74–91 by Kim Kissling
All recipes developed by Brigit Binns except the following:
pages 76–90